# CHIC DECOR DESIGN HOUSE

We hope you enjoy your décor book and the beauty it offers to your space.

Explore other titles in the BEACH HOUSE SERIES for complimenting books.

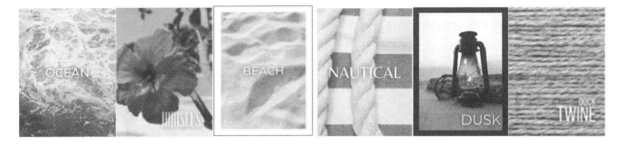

Create your own unique look by mixing and matching with popular titles from our other series:

## DESIGNER BLACK&WHITE SERIES

## ALOHA SERIES

## WOODLAND NATURE SERIES

If this book added the perfect touch to your interior design plan, we would be thankful if you could take a quick moment to leave your Amazon Review.

Questions and comments are welcome at chicdecordesignhouse@gmail.com

Made in the USA
Monee, IL
04 February 2024